WHAT'S YOUR PERFECT VACATION?

By Brooke Rowe

Published in the United States of America by Cherry Lake Publishing
Ann Arbor, Michigan
www.cherrylakepublishing.com

Reading Adviser: Marla Conn, ReadAbility, Inc.
Book Designer: Melinda Millward

Photo Credits: © William Perugini/Shutterstock.com, back cover, 4; © monkeybusinessimages/Thinkstock.com, back cover, 4; © Oleg Kozlov/Shutterstock Images, cover, 1, 30; © Zurijeta/Shutterstock Images, 6; © CandyBox Images/Shutterstock Images, 6; © Lopolo/Shutterstock Images, 7; © michaeljung/Thinkstock.com, 7; © Csehak Szabolcs/Shutterstock Images, 8; © omgimages/Thinkstock.com, 8; © Daniel Bendjy/Thinkstock.com, 9; © Digital Vision/Thinkstock.com, 9; © Dan Holm / Shutterstock.com, 10; © Marko Poplasen/Shutterstock Images, 10; © arek_malang/Shutterstock Images, 11; ©Samuel Borges Photography/Shutterstock Images, 11; © Dragon Images/Shutterstock Images, 12; © wavebreakmedia/Shutterstock Images, 12; © Monkey Business Images/Shutterstock Images, 13; © KieferPix/Shutterstock Images, 13; © Denis Burdin/Shutterstock Images, 14; © roman_Slavik/Thinkstock.com, 14; © Catarina Belova / Shutterstock.com, 15; © Poprotskiy Alexey/Shutterstock Images, 15; © Andrey_Popov/Shutterstock Images, 16; © IT Stock Free/Thinkstock.com, 16; © Dudarev Mikhail/Shutterstock Images, 17; © Teri Virbickis/Shutterstock Images, 17; © Paolo Schorli/Shutterstock Images, 18; © solominviktor/Shutterstock Images, 18; © oliveromg/Shutterstock Images, 19; © Phase4Studios/Shutterstock Images, 19; © Pindiyath100 | Dreamstime.com - Disney Pixar Finding Nemo Character Photo, 20; © Clewisleake | Dreamstime.com - Disney\'s Princess Elsa From Frozen At Disneyworld Photo, 20; © Ramblingsmummy | Dreamstime.com - Toy Story, Buzz Lightyear And Woody On A Float At Disneyland Paris Photo, 21; © s_bukley / Shutterstock.com, 21; © ollyiaa/Deposit Photos, 22; © BMJ/Shutterstock Images, 22; © Can Stock Photo Inc. / Dorian2013, 23; © lauraslens/Shutterstock Images, 23; © Germanskydiver/Shutterstock Images, 24; © Alex Nabokov/Shutterstock Images, 24; © michaeljung/Shutterstock Images, 25; © 06photo/Shutterstock Images, 25; © bernashafo/Shutterstock Images, 26; © Jasmine_K/Shutterstock Images, 26; © Smit/Shutterstock Images, 27; © el lobo/Shutterstock Images, 27; © Andrey_Kuzmin/Shutterstock Images, 28; © Purestock/Thinkstock.com, 28; © Olena Brodetska/Shutterstock Images, 29; © Green Jo/Shutterstock Images, 29; © NAN728/Shutterstock Images, 30; © Racheal Grazias/Shutterstock Images, 31; © Jaroslava V/Shutterstock Images, 31

Graphic Element Credits: © Silhouette Lover/Shutterstock Images, back cover, multiple interior pages; © Arevik/Shutterstock Images, back cover, multiple interior pages; © tukkki/Shutterstock Images, multiple interior pages; © paprika/Shutterstock Images, 24

45th Parallel Press is an imprint of Cherry Lake Publishing.

CIP data has been filed and is available at catalog.loc.gov.

Printed in the United States of America
Corporate Graphics

Table of Contents

Hey! Welcome to the Best Quiz Ever series. This is a book. Duh. But it's also a pretty awesome quiz. Don't worry. It's not about math. Or history. Or anything you might get graded on. Snooze.

This is a quiz all about YOU.

To Take the Best Quiz Ever:

Answer honestly!
Keep track of your answers. But don't write in the book!
(Hint: Make a copy of this handy chart.)
Don't see the answer you want? Pick the closest one.
Take it alone. Take it with friends!
Have fun! Obviously.

Question 1 _____   Question 7 _____

Question 2 _____   Question 8 _____

Question 3 _____   Question 9 _____

Question 4 _____   Question 10 _____

Question 5 _____   Question 11 _____

Question 6 _____   Question 12 _____

What note gets written most on your report card?

A. Falls asleep in class!

B. Forgets to do homework!

C. Too busy!

D. Talks too much!

Did you know?

*Eating foods with **cinnamon** can help improve your memory.*

Your favorite outfit includes:

A. A bathing suit and flip-flops

B. A cozy sweater

C. Layers. So easy!

D. Shorts and a hoodie

Did you know?

The oldest pair of flip-flops are from between 1550 and 1307 BCE.

What item is always in your backpack?

A. Sunnies

B. My pass for the skate park

C. Camera

D. Cell phone

Did you know?
One of the first skate parks opened
in Tucson, Arizona, in 1965.

You wouldn't be caught dead _____:

A. Running a marathon

B. At the mall on Saturday

C. Without a **passport**

D. At the library by myself

Did you know?

A marathon is 26.2 miles (42 kilometers) long. The man who ran the first recorded marathon died when he finished.

What continent seems like the most fun?

A. North America

B. Antarctica

C. Africa? Asia? Just one?!

D. South America. Brazil, baby!

Did you know?
Only about 10 babies have been born in Antarctica.

Choose a travel bag:

A. Beach bag

B. Waterproof duffle

C. Rolling suitcase

D. Backpacking bag

Did you know?
Ducks have waterproof feathers.

A walk on a sandy beach sounds:

A. Like heaven

B. Boring

18

C. Great! But not too long!

D. How many friends are with me?

Did you know?

"Wild beaches" are beaches that hardly anyone knows about. There are no crowds or buildings.

What's your favorite Disney movie?

A. Finding Nemo

B. Frozen

C. *Monsters University*

D. *Toy Story*

Did you know?
Clown fish, like Nemo, live in the
Indian and Pacific Oceans.

The WORST family vacation would be:

A. Hiking

B. Going to Disney World

C. Visiting the same place as last year

D. Going to the beach. Again.

Did you know?
The first Disney World opened in Florida in 1971.

Your best friend calls you:

A. Easygoing

B. Adventurous

C. Ambitious

D. At least five times a day

Did you know?
The first cell phone was made by Motorola in 1973.

You're painting your room. What color?

A. Light blue

B. Bright purple

C. Forest green

D. Yellow

Did you know?

It takes 555 pounds (252 kilograms)
of paint to paint a 747 airplane.

Pick a pet:

A. A cat

B. A husky

C. A fish

D. A golden retriever

Did you know?

Hundreds of years ago, Chinese royalty kept goldfish as pets.

You're done! Now you tally your score. Add up your As, Bs, Cs, and Ds. What letter do you have the most of? BTW, if you have a tie, you're a little bit of both.

As: Caribbean Cruise

You love splashing in the waves. And catching rays. And generally relaxing in the heat. You've been called lazy. But you really just like to stop and smell the roses. Your perfect vacation is a Caribbean cruise! You would love the onboard activities. You would love the stops at island beaches. And bonus: packing is easy! Just a bathing suit and sunscreen!

Bs: Dogsledding

You have always been a bit odd. In a good way! You march to a different drummer. You love the snow. And bundling up for cold weather. You're always up for an adventure—with luck, one that no one has been on yet! You should go on a dogsledding vacation! You'll have fun racing through the snowy woods with a pack of dogs!

Cs: African Safari

You want to see the world! You want to mark all the places you've visited on a map. France. Hong Kong. Australia. You want to see it all! You should start with the trip of a lifetime. Your dream vacation is an African safari! You will see a totally new and different country. Plus you'll get to check out animals most people only get to see at zoos! But remember, "Don't feed the animals!"

Ds: Amusement Park

A great vacation would be racing from ride to ride at an amusement park. With a bunch of friends! Disneyland. The Wizarding World of Harry Potter. Six Flags. They all sound awesome! You'll be the one chowing snacks from the snack bar. And riding the newest (scariest) rides. You've been called a daredevil. But you would love to have some thrilling fun with friends.

Glossary

ambitious (am-BISH-uhs) having a strong desire to do well

cinnamon (SIN-uh-muhn) a spice that comes from the bark of a tropical tree

hike (hike) a long walk in the country or mountains

husky (HUHS-kee) a strong dog with a thick coat, bred to pull sleds in the snow

passport (PAS-port) an official document that says you are a citizen of a certain country

waterproof (WAW-tur-proof) something that does not allow water to enter

Index